West Coast

12

Jocey Asnong

RMB

One lighthouse on a windswept coast

Sooke

1

2

Two orcas breach our boat

Great Bear Rainforest

3

Three spirit bears balance on a cedar tree

Four dolphins show off favourite flips

Flores Island

4

Five divers
find a surprise

Valdez Island

5

Six seals soak up the sun

6

Sidney·by·the·Sea

Seven boarders carve through a snow bowl

Whistler Blackcomb

7

Eight kayaks explore the shore

Cowichan Bay

8

Nine boats sail
by coast line

9

Desolation Sound

Ten hikers follow a trail through the rainforest

West coast Trail

11

**Eleven geese
go sightseeing**

**Twelve
sea wolves
swim across
the cove**

12

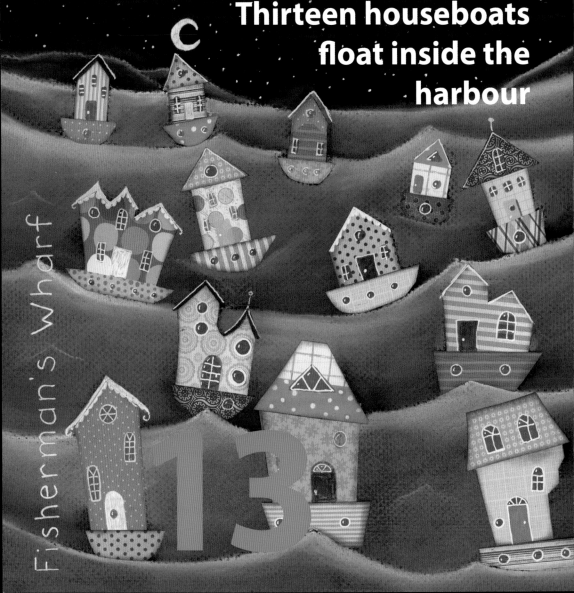

Thirteen houseboats float inside the harbour

Fisherman's Wharf

13

Fourteen surfers rip through curls

Tofino

14

Fifteen frogs sing in the fog

Comox Lake

15

16

Sixteen salmon spawn upstream

Squamish River

17

Seventeen shells for us to collect

Eighteen mushrooms grow among the evergreens

Nineteen bees
help flowers bloom

19

Butchart Gardens

20

Twenty
starfish
tickle
our toes

Haida Gwaii

JOCEY ASNONG was raised by a pack of wild pencil crayons in a house made out of paper and stories. After finishing several years of illustration school at Sheridan College, she left the land of maple trees in Ontario and moved to the mountains of Alberta so she could wear mittens most of the year. When she is not chasing her cats around her art cave in Canmore, she might be caught in a blizzard near Mount Everest, or running away from wild dogs in Mongolia, or peeking out castle windows in Scotland, or sleeping under the stars in Bolivia. Jocey's books for children include *Nuptse and Lhotse in Nepal*, *Nuptse and Lhotse Go to the Rockies*, *Nuptse and Lhotse Go to Iceland*, *Nuptse and Lhotse Go to the West Coast*, *Rocky Mountain ABCs*, *Rocky Mountain 123s*, *West Coast ABCs*, and *West Coast 123s*.

1 2 3 4 5 6 7

8 9 10 11 12

13 14 15 16

17 18 19 20

For information on purchasing bulk quantities of this book, or to obtain media excerpts or invite the author to speak at an event, please visit rmbooks.com and select the "Contact" tab.

RMB | Rocky Mountain Books Ltd.
rmbooks.com
@rmbooks
facebook.com/rmbooks

Cataloguing data available from Library and Archives Canada
ISBN 9781771603027 (board book)
ISBN 9781771605045 (softcover)

Design by Chyla Cardinal

Printed and bound in China by 1010 Printing International Ltd.

We would like to also take this opportunity to acknowledge the traditional territories upon which we live, work, and play. In Calgary, Alberta, we acknowledge the Niitsitapi (Blackfoot) and the people of the Treaty 7 region in Southern Alberta, which includes the Siksika, the Piikuni, the Kainai, the Tsuut'ina and the Stoney Nakoda First Nations, including Chiniki, Bearpaw, and Wesley First Nations. The City of Calgary is also home to Métis Nation of Alberta, Region III. In Victoria, British Columbia, we acknowledge the traditional territories of the Lkwungen (Esquimalt, and Songhees), Malahat, Pacheedaht, Scia'new, T'Sou-ke and W̱SÁNEĆ (Pauquachin, Tsartlip, Tsawout, Tseycum) peoples.

We acknowledge the financial support of the Government of Canada through the Canada Book Fund and the Canada Council for the Arts, and of the province of British Columbia through the British Columbia Arts Council and the Book Publishing Tax Credit.

Disclaimer
The views expressed in this book are those of the author and do not necessarily reflect those of the publishing company, its staff, or its affiliates.